Snake Stuff!

Hiya, I'm Zeek.

Hi, I'm Finn.

Calling all aliens!
Are you planning a holiday to planet Earth?
Finn and Zeek are here to help.

'Snake Stuff!'
Published by MAVERICK ARTS PUBLISHING LTD

Suite 1, Hillreed House, 54 Queen Street,
Horsham, RH13 5AD +44 (0)1403 256941
© Maverick Arts Publishing Limited August 2024

A CIP catalogue record for this book is available at the British Library.

ISBN 978-1-83511-011-9

Printed in India

www.maverickbooks.co.uk

Credits:

Finn & Zeek illustrations by Jake McDonald, Bright Illustration Agency
Cover: Jake McDonald/Bright, © Tanto Yensen/Shutterstock
Inside: © Eric Isselee/Shutterstock (6), © Cheng Wei/Shutterstock (7), © Martin Pelanek/Shutterstock (8), © Rich Carey/Shutterstock (8), © objectsforall/Shutterstock (10-11), © Aaron of L.A. Photography/Shutterstock (12), © Ondrej Prosicky/Shutterstock (12), © COULANGES/Shutterstock (13), © Stanislav Duben/Shutterstock (14), © Jannarong/Shutterstock (14), © Eric Isselee/Shutterstock (15), © Skynavin/Shutterstock (16), © Rich Carey/Shutterstock (16), © Cede Prudente/iStock by Getty Images (17), © ROSA ROMERO HERRERA/Shutterstock (18-19), © Dr Morley Read/Shutterstock (20), © Nynke van Holten/Shutterstock (20-21), © Roberto 33/Shutterstock (22), © chomplearn/Shutterstock (23), © Alex James Bramwell/Shutterstock (24), © Kurit afshen/Shutterstock (25), © Ixepop/Shutterstock (25), © Kurit afshen/Shutterstock (27), © Kurit afshen/Shutterstock (29)

This book is rated as: Orange Band (Guided Reading)
It follows the requirements for Phase 5 phonics.
Most words are decodable, and any non-decodable words are familiar, supported by the context and/or represented in the artwork.

Snake Stuff!

Contents

Introduction	6
Snake Habitats	8
A Snake's Body	10
Snake Babies!	13
Scales and Skin	14
How They Get About	16
Dinner Time!	18
Big and Small	20
Scary Snakes?	22
Sneaky Snakes	24
Safe Snakes?	25
Quiz	28
Index/Glossary	30

INCOMING MESSAGE

Dear Finn and Zeek,

We are planning a holiday on Earth. We would love to know more about snakes. Can you tell us about them?

Thank you!

From,
Hed and Tal *(Planet Serp)*

Introduction

Snakes belong to a group of animals called reptiles. Other reptiles include lizards and crocodiles.

Snakes are **vertebrates**, which means they have a backbone. Here's the skeleton of a python:

There are over 3000 kinds of snake in the world!

Snake Habitats

Some snakes live on the land...

Smooth snake

...and some even live in the sea!

Banded sea krait

There are snakes in most places but not Antarctica (it is too cold), Ireland and a few other places!

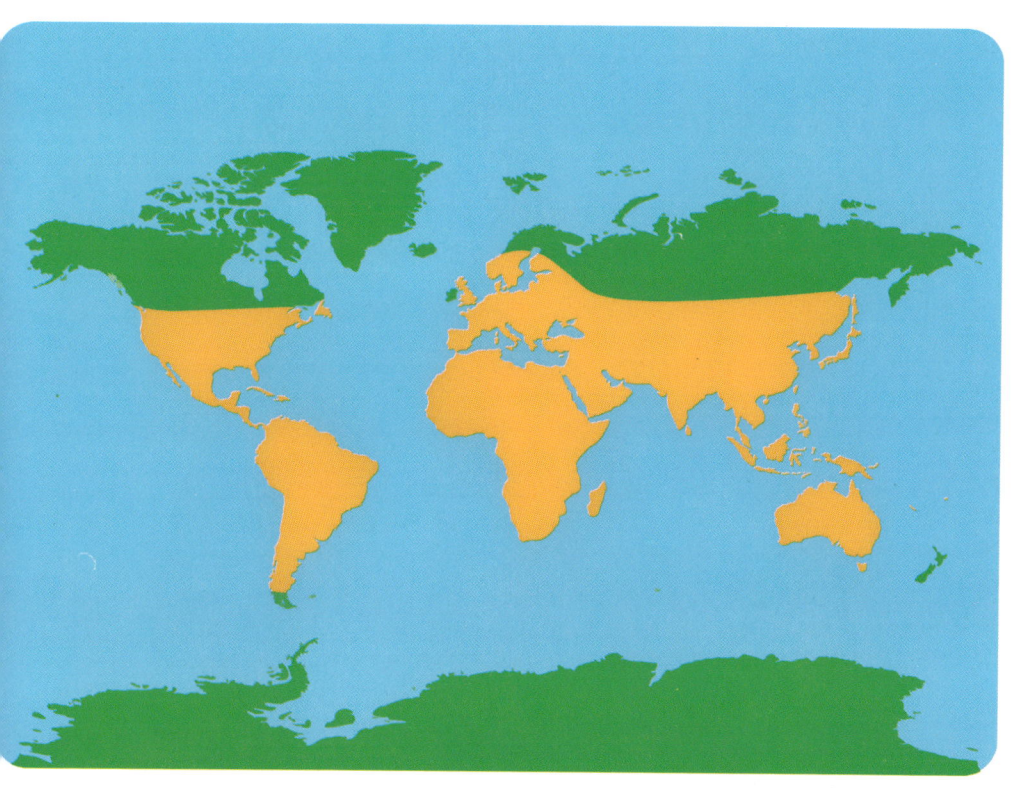

Above is a world map.

■ Green = No snakes

■ Yellow = You can find snakes

A Snake's Body

How are snakes different from us?

They don't have ears! They have a special bone that helps them to hear.

Snakes don't have legs!

Boa snake

They don't have eyelids and sleep with their eyes open.

They can even smell with their tongues.

I bet you can't do that!

A Snake's Body

Snakes feel hot or cold based on the temperature around them. They are **cold-blooded**.

Common garter

Adder

Humans are **warm-blooded**, which means we can control our body temperatures from the inside.

Snake Babies!

Most snakes lay eggs which baby snakes hatch from.

Burmese python

Some snakes give birth to live young (like humans).

Scales and Skin

Most snakes have scales. Some use their scales to hold on to surfaces and help them climb.

Ball python

Viperine

Snakes shed their skin head-first!

As they grow bigger, snakes get rid of their old skin and grow a new one! This is called shedding.

How They Get About

Most snakes slither across the ground or climb trees.

Cobra

But some snakes can swim. Most sea snakes can only travel underwater.

Banded sea krait

Dinner Time!

Most snakes eat their food without chewing.

Snakes usually eat small animals like mice, birds, frogs and bugs. But big snakes can eat larger animals like monkeys!

Big and Small

The smallest known snake is the Barbados thread snake. The longest it grows to is 10cm!

Thread snake
(not to scale)

10cm*

* Approximately

Reticulated pythons are the longest type of snake. They can grow over 6m long! That's roughly the length of 60 Barbados thread snakes lying head to tail!

Reticulated python
(not to scale)

Scary Snakes?

Some snakes, like king cobras, are **venomous**. They attack their prey with **toxic** venom and use it to defend themselves.

king cobra

Venomous snakes can be dangerous to humans. But some types of venom can also be used to make medicine for people!

Sneaky Snakes

Non-venomous snakes have other ways of hunting.

Snakes like boa constrictors can squeeze their prey to death.

Safe Snakes?

Corn snake

Most kinds of snake are non-venomous and of little danger to humans! However, always check with an expert before touching one.

MESSAGE SENT

Dear Hed and Tal,

You can see that snakes are wonderful animals! There are so many different kinds of snake. We like the ones that can fly best!

Have fun on Earth!

From,
Finn and Zeek :)

Here's a blue snake, called a blue viper!

Quiz

1. Which group of animals do snakes belong to?
a) Mammals
b) Insects
c) Reptiles

2. What can snakes smell with?
a) Their ears
b) Their tongues
c) Their eyes

3. Snakes are...
a) cold-blooded
b) hot-blooded
c) warm-blooded

4. What is it called when snakes lose their old skin?
a) Skinning
b) Slimming
c) Shedding

5. Where do most snakes live?
a) On land
b) In the sea
c) In the air

6. What type of snake is this?
a) Boa constrictor
b) Cobra
c) Corn snake

Turn over for answers

Index/Glossary

Cold-blooded pg 12
Animals which feel hot or cold based on the temperature around them.

Reticulated pg 21
A pattern that looks like a net.

Toxic pg 22
Something that is poisonous or harmful.

Venomous pg 22, 23, 24, 25
When something makes venom (a toxic liquid).

Vertebrates pg 7
Animals which have a backbone.

Quiz Answers:

1. c, 2. b, 3. a, 4. c, 5. a, 6. c

Warm-blooded pg 12
Animals which can control their body temperature from the inside.

Book Bands for Guided Reading

The Institute of Education book banding system is a scale of colours that reflects the various levels of reading difficulty. The bands are assigned by taking into account the content, the language style, the layout and phonics. Word, phrase and sentence level work is also taken into consideration.

Maverick Early Readers are a bright, attractive range of books covering the pink to white bands. All of these books have been book banded for guided reading to the industry standard and edited by a leading educational consultant.

Fiction

Non-fiction

To view the whole Maverick Readers scheme, visit our website at www.maverickearlyreaders.com

Or scan the QR code above to view our scheme instantly!

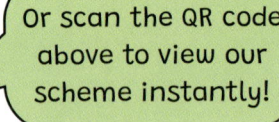